250

Would You Rather Questions

A Clean, Fun and Hilarious
Activity Book for Kids,
Teens and Adults

How To Play

Step 1

Split into two teams whether that be boys vs girls, kids vs parents, or any other mix of your choice. If possible, also assign one person as a referee.

Step 2

Decide who gets to go first. Which team can do the most pushups? Which team can guess the number between 1 and 10 from someone not playing the game? Or just a good old-fashioned rock paper scissors?

Step 3

The starting team must ask a question from the book and the opposing team has 10 seconds to not only choose an option but to also give a meaningful reason as to why they chose what they did. The referee decides whether the answer is acceptable.

Step 4

The team can discuss their answer together but only one player can give the answer. The person answering must alternate every turn.

Step 5

If the player who is answering can't choose or give a good reason, then that player is out for the game and can't answer anymore or be involved in the team discussion.

Step 6

Repeat until all players are eliminated.

Questions

1. Would you rather live one life that lasts **1000** years or **10** lives that last **100** years each?

2. Would you rather use eye drops made of vinegar or toilet paper made of sandpaper?

3. Would you rather be 4'0 or 8'0?

4. Would you rather be super strong or super fast?

5. Would you rather take a guaranteed $120,000 or take a 50/50 chance at $1,000,000?

6. Would you rather be in constant pain or have a constant itch?

7. Would you rather go forward or backward in time?

8. Would you rather never be able to take a hot shower again or eat hot food again?

9. Would you rather never play or play but always lose?

10. Would you rather be a vegetarian or only be able to eat meat?

11. Would you rather be a chronic farter or chronic burper?

12. Would you rather be deaf or mute?

13. Would you rather have a third eye or third arm?

14. Would you rather age from the neck up only or neck down only?

15. Would you rather be only able to shout or whisper?

16. Would you rather never touch an electronic device again or a human?

17. Would you rather have a mediocre short term memory or bad long term memory?

18. Would you rather have 2 wishes today or 3 wishes in 5 years?

19. Would you rather drink a glass of expired milk or pee your pants in public?

20. Would you rather hang out with a few friends or go to a big party?

21. Would you rather master every language or every instrument?

22. Would you rather have to wear formal clothes for the rest of your life or informal?

23. Would you rather eat a stick of butter or a teaspoon of cinnamon?

24. Would you rather have the ability to read people's minds or fly?

25. Would you rather have your house always have its lights on or off?

26. Would you rather be ignorant and happy or knowledgeable but not content?

27. Would you rather have to take cold showers to be clean or never be clean at all?

28. Would you rather lick someone's armpit or lick your floor?

29. Would you rather have your flight be delayed by 18 hours or lose your luggage?

30. Would you rather be an amazing player on the losing team or the worst player on the winning team?

31. Would you rather be ugly and marry a good looking person or be good looking and marry an ugly person?

32. Would you rather be a genius in a world of morons or a moron in a world of geniuses?

33. Would you rather be stuck in a house alone or with someone you hate?

34. Would you rather dump someone or have them dump you?

35. Would you rather be a parent or child?

36. Would you rather lose your arms or legs?

37. Would you rather be homeless for a year or go to jail for a year?

38. Would you rather go without the internet for a month or transportation?

39. Would you rather be homeless or be without family and friends?

40. Would you rather be really hairy or completely bald?

41. Would you rather eat healthy or exercise every day?

42. Would you rather lose half your hearing or half your hair?

43. Would you rather look weak and actually be strong or look strong and actually be weak?

44. Would you rather be miserable but rich at a job or love what you do but be poor?

45. Would you rather be rich and ugly or poor and good looking?

46. Would you rather be in constant pain or have a constant itch?

47. Would you rather be unable to ask questions or unable to give any answers?

48. Would you rather save the life of someone close to you or 7 random strangers?

49. Would you rather have a dragon or be a dragon?

50. Would you rather be literate or be able to read minds and be illiterate?

51. Would you rather be able to speak every language or be the best at something in the world?

52. Would you rather wear really warm clothes in the desert or no clothes in the Arctic?

53. Would you rather be able to change the past or future?

54. Would you rather never use a car again or your cellphone?

55. Would you rather lose $1000 or all your phone contacts?

56. Would you rather be stung by 3 bees or give up your phone for a week?

57. Would you rather give up **TV** for the rest of your life or coffee?

58. Would you rather win a trip to an exotic destination or a new **TV**?

59. Would you rather give up ice cream or pizza?

60. Would you rather eat your boogers or lick the bottom of your shoe?

61. Would you rather be a police officer or a firefighter?

62. Would you rather have smelly feet or bad breath?

63. Would you rather be the smartest kid in school or the most popular?

64. Would you rather be on a survival game show or a dating game show?

65. Would you rather end war or world hunger?

66. Would you rather be Batman or Superman?

67. Would you rather read books or watch movies?

68. Would you rather never have to pay for clothes again or food?

69. Would you rather go on a blind date or date someone you met online?

70. Would you rather be an unknown NBA player or a badminton star?

71. Would you rather go to an amusement park or a beach?

72. Would you rather be able to talk with animals or speak all languages?

73. Would you rather win the lottery or live an extra 15 years?

74. Would you rather have x ray vision or enhanced hearing?

75. Would you rather have to sew your own clothes or grow your own food?

76. Would you rather have **Rambo** or the **Terminator** as your bodyguard?

77. Would you rather have the details of your love life or financial life to be made public?

78. Would you rather be gossiped about or never talked about at all?

79. Would you rather have a family of 12 children or none at all?

80. Would you rather be an adult your whole life or a kid?

81. Would you rather give up watching TV/movies or games for a year?

82. Would you rather be able to see what was behind every closed door or know the passcode to every safe?

83. Would you rather always be able to see 5 minutes into the future or 100 years into the future?

84. Would you rather have unlimited first class tickets for travelling or never have to pay for food at restaurants again?

85. Would you rather be balding and super fit with a six pack or have a full set of hair and be slightly overweight?

86. Would you rather have super sensitive taste or super sensitive hearing?

87. Would you rather have Christmas be cold and snowy or hot and sunny?

88. Would you rather swap your feet for wheels or your hands for knives?

89. Would you rather have a real or fake Christmas tree?

90. Would you rather clean the floor with a toothbrush or mow the yard with a pair of scissors?

91. Would you rather make a small difference in the lives of 10 people or a big difference in one person's life?

92. Would you rather eat shrimp covered in candy or oatmeal with onions in it?

93. Would you rather drink orange juice or apple juice?

94. Would you rather own a Lamborghini or Ferrari?

95. Would you rather not shower for a month or not change your clothes for a month?

96. Would you rather have a stone in your shoe or an eyelash in your eye?

97. Would you rather save money or spend it?

98. Would you rather be trapped in a room for an hour full of mosquitoes or rats?

99. Would you rather go to a water park or an amusement park?

100. Would you rather receive 5 anonymous Valentine's day gifts or receive one but know who it was from?

101. Would you rather have your best friend be a girl or guy?

102. Would you rather have your sibling throw sand in your eye or have them give you a wedgie?

103. Would you rather work on a cruise ship or on an airplane?

104. Would you rather have a green or yellow car?

105. Would you rather have purple or yellow hair?

106. Would you rather go to school or work?

107. Would you rather be bitten by a shark or attacked by a swarm of bees?

108. Would you rather have no exams for the rest of your life or no homework?

109. Would you rather have a time machine or the ability to fly?

110. Would you rather swim with dolphins or ride an elephant?

111. Would you rather listen to the same song for 100 hours straight or listen to no music for a month?

112. Would you rather shop online or in a physical store?

113. Would you rather give a speech to a crowd or perform a dance?

114. Would you rather take 1 vacation that lasts 4 weeks or 4 vacations that last 1 week each?

115. Would you rather eat no candy on Halloween or no turkey on Thanksgiving?

116. Would you feel worse if no one showed up to your birthday or funeral?

117. Would you rather have a desk job or outdoor/physically engaging job?

118. Would you rather hear the good news or bad news first?

119. Would you rather have nosy neighbors or noisy neighbors?

120. Would you rather live the rest of your life in solitary as a monk or always be followed around by paparazzi?

121. Would you rather go into the past and meet your ancestors or go into the future and meet your great-great-great grandchildren?

122. Would you rather spend a night in a hotel room or out in a tent while camping?

123. Would you rather be an Olympian gold medalist or a Nobel Prize winner?

124. Would you rather be too busy or too bored?

125. Would you rather live in the Sahara or Antarctica?

126. Would you rather have your first child when you are 18 or 40?

127. Would you rather spend the day with your favorite athlete or your favorite movie star?

128. Would you rather wear uniforms to school or have clothing of your choice?

129. Would you rather be part of an arranged marriage or spend your life single?

130. Would you rather be known for your good looks or your intelligence?

131. Would you rather be able to detect any lie you hear or get away with any lie you tell?

132. Would you rather drink a glass of spit or a glass of snot?

133. Would you rather be a hopeless romantic or hopeful unromantic?

134. Would you rather have too many friends or too few?

135. Would you rather find true love or be rich?

136. Would you rather create history or delete it?

137. Would you rather eat your friend's scab or lick the bottom of both of their feet?

138. Would you rather become famous or powerful?

139. Would you rather be a creative person or technical person?

140. Would you rather get a papercut every time you touched paper or bite your tongue every time you ate food?

141. Would you rather wake up in the morning looking like a giraffe or kangaroo?

142. Would you rather eat a small can of dog food or a somewhat moldy banana?

143. Would you rather drink all the half finished drinks at a party or the half finished food?

144. Would you rather be able to speak to dolphins or read babies' minds?

145. Would you rather have two permanent lazy eyes or always get nosebleeds at embarrassing moments?

146. Would you rather sound like Jar-Jar Binks for the rest of your life or Siri?

147. Would you rather have your name be Little Caesar or Domino?

148. Would you rather eat pizza everyday or never be able to eat ever again?

149. Would you rather always get stuck in traffic or always have a really slow internet connection?

150. Would you rather have to hunt and make your own food for the rest of your life or eat only McDonald's?

151. Would you rather have a higher IQ or photographic memory?

152. If you had $500,000, would you rather spend it all or invest it all?

153. Would you rather have a missing finger or two extra fingers?

154. Would you rather talk like Yoda or breathe like Darth Vader?

155. Would you rather be forced to wear wet socks forever or only be allowed to wash your hair once a year?

156. Would you rather have $1,000,000 now or $5,000 per week for the rest of your life?

157. Would you rather have great friends or a great significant other?

158. Would you rather have a rich, dumb, good looking significant

other or an average looking, poor, caring significant other?

159. Would you rather have your employer or your parents go through your text messages?

160. Would you rather date someone that gets along with your friends or family?

161. Would you rather be the life of the party or invisible during it?

162. Would you rather receive a gift made by hand or one that's bought?

163. Would you rather know how you will die or when you will die?

164. Would you rather have free Wi-Fi wherever you went or free coffee?

165. Would you rather be able to talk your way out of any situation or fight your way?

166. Would you rather have 3 kids and $30,000 or not have the ability to have kids but have $3,000,000?

167. Would you rather be famous when you are alive but forgotten when you die or vice versa?

168. Would you rather have your shirts be two sizes too big or one size too small?

169. Would you rather live far from civilization or live in civilization as a homeless person?

170. Would you rather have the public be proud of you but your family think you're horrible or vice versa?

171. Would you rather live in virtual reality where you're a king or in the real world?

172. Would you rather have an easy job working for someone else or a

hard job but you work for
yourself?

173. Would you rather be the
discoverer of a planet or the
inventor of a medicine that cures
a deadly disease?

174. Would you rather have a terrible
job but be able to retire within 5
years or have a great job but retire
in 25 years?

175. Would you rather be able to
teleport or read minds?

176. Would you rather die in 20 years
with no regrets or in 50 years
with regrets?

177. Would you rather be feared or loved?

178. Would you rather be able to control fire or water?

179. Would you rather have all your food be too salty or not salty enough?

180. Would you rather have big hands or big feet?

181. Would you rather go back 5 years with everything you know now or know everything your future self knows now?

182. Would you rather be able to control machines or animals with your mind?

183. Would you rather sell all of your possessions or one of your organs?

184. Would you rather lose all your memories from birth to now or not have the ability to form new ones from now on?

185. Would you rather be held in high regard by your parents or friends?

186. Would you rather be an amazing painter or an amazing mathematician?

187. Would you rather be reincarnated as a fly or cease to exist?

188. Would you rather have everyone laugh at your jokes but not find anyone else's funny or you find everyone's jokes funny but no one laugh at your jokes?

189. Would you rather go to the moon or mars?

190. Would you rather fight 100 duck sized horses or 1 horse sized duck?

191. Would you rather have your breath smell like a fart or your laugh sound like a fart?

192. Would you rather get even or get over it?

193. Would you rather be super strong or have the ability to change into different animals?

194. Would you rather sound like Mickey Mouse or Donald Duck for the rest of your life?

195. Would you rather fight Mike Tyson or talk like him forever?

196. Would you rather be the villain or the hero?

197. Would you rather win an Olympic gold medal or an Oscar?

198. Would you rather have food stuck in your two front teeth when you smile at someone or a booger in one nostril?

199. Would you rather play video games or play outside?

200. Would you rather live in Narnia or go to school at Hogwarts?

201. Would you rather have a nice house and an ugly car or a nice car and an ugly house?

202. Would you rather date someone 10 years older or 10 years younger?

203. Would you rather borrow $1000 from your parents or from your friends?

204. Would you rather be very strong or be able to run very fast?

205. Would you rather go skiing in the winter or to the beach in summer?

206. Would you rather have straight hair or curly hair?

207. Would you rather be extremely afraid of heights or of water?

208. Would you rather be a legendary singer or a legendary guitar player?

209. Would you rather have your emails of the last month be read by everyone or your texts from the last week?

210. Would you rather be a tiger or a lion?

211. Would you rather be shot out of a cannon or stick your head in a lion's mouth?

212. Would you rather lose all your keys or your phone?

213. Would you rather go back and prevent the sinking of the **Titanic** or the **Great Depression**?

214. Would you rather do laundry or clean dishes?

215. Would you rather be stuck in a submarine at the bottom of the ocean or in a space shuttle in space?

216. Would you rather live with someone you hate for the rest of your life or completely alone?

217. Would you rather save the life of an elderly family member or a child that you don't know?

218. Would you rather spend a year in a mental asylum or a year in jail?

219. Would you rather share a toothbrush with a stranger or kiss them?

220. Would you rather be completely alone for 5 years or never alone for 5 years?

221. Would you rather have a skinny upper body but muscular lower body or a muscular upper body and a skinny lower body?

222. Would you rather make double your pay while working or have a year off and get paid your normal salary?

223. Would you rather stand all day or sit?

224. Would you rather be an employee or own your own business?

225. Would you rather have 500 spiders in your room or 1000 cockroaches in your house?

226. Would you rather eat a dead bug or lick a worm?

227. Would you rather be weak but have lots of stamina or strong but have little stamina?

228. Would you rather be a superhero or a wizard?

229. Would you rather be a masculine female or a feminine male?

230. Would you rather eat a whole jar of mayonnaise or margarine?

231. Would you rather live in the White House or in Buckingham Palace?

232. Would you rather have a runny nose for the rest of your life or cough every time after every word you spoke?

233. Would you rather have your brain transplanted into a robot or an animal?

234. Would you rather get attacked by zombies or by sharks?

235. Would you rather always forget who you are or who everyone else is?

236. Would you rather feel like you need to sneeze but not be able to for the rest of your life or have hiccups for the rest of your life?

237. Would you rather go to Hogwarts but be a muggle or live in a world of Pokemon but only be able to catch Magikarps?

238. Would you rather eat a hotdog with a hamburger bun or a hamburger with a hot dog bun?

239. Would you rather sleep in as late as you want or stay up for last as you want?

240. Would you rather be a surgeon or a dentist?

241. Would you rather have a dog or a cat?

242. Would you rather have $10 million in 10 years from now or $1 million today?

243. Would you rather always be 10 minutes late or 20 minutes early?

244. Would you rather win $50,000 or let your best friend win $500,000?

245. Would you rather visit Italy or Spain?

246. Would you rather wear clown makeup for a year or a pink tutu for a year?

247. For one month, would you rather be vegan or only be able to eat meat and dairy?

248. Would you rather live in a house without water or a house without power?

249. Would you rather be able to copy and paste in real life or undo?

250. Would you rather be able to lift up to 100 lbs with your mind or 1,000 normally?

Thank you for reading! We hope everyone enjoyed the book, and had lots of fun and laughs.

As a special bonus, enjoy this exclusive preview of one our other popular titles!

Would You Rather

EWW GROSS!
Edition

How to Play

Step 1

Split into two teams whether that be boys vs girls, kids vs parents, or any mix of your choice. If possible, also assign one person as a referee.

Step 2

Decide who gets to go first. Which team can do the most pushups? Which team can guess the number between 1 and 10 from someone not playing the game? Or just some good old fashioned rock paper scissors?

Step 3

The starting team has to ask a question from the book and the opposing team has 10 seconds to not only choose an option but to also give a meaningful reason as to why they chose what they did. The referee decides whether the answer is acceptable.

Step 4

The team can discuss their answer together but only one player can give the answer. The person answering has to alternate every turn.

Step 5

If the player who is answering can't choose or give a good reason then that player is out for the game and can't answer anymore or be involved in the team discussion.

Step 6

Repeat until all players are eliminated.

Let's begin!

Would You Rather...

Drink someone else's pee

-OR-

eat your own poo?

Let someone fart on your face

-OR-

punch you in the face?

Would You Rather...

Eat bugs for breakfast

-OR-

give up your top 3 foods?

Eat a popcorn bag filled with dead flies

-OR-

be surrounded by flies for a month?

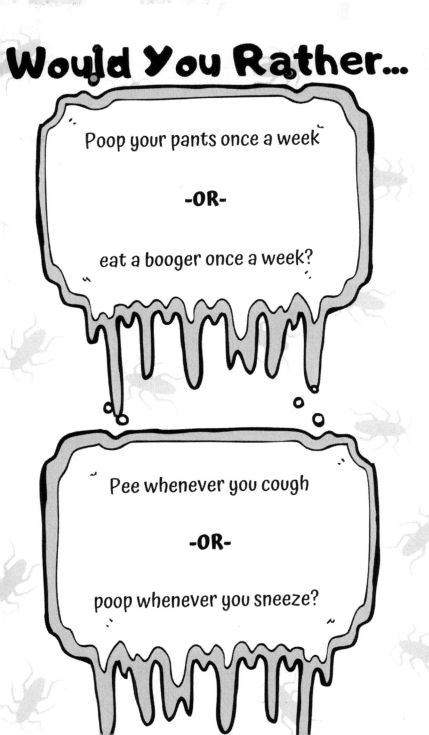

A Message From the Publisher

Hello! My name is Hayden and I am the owner of Hayden Fox Publishing, the publishing house that brought you this title.

My hope is that you enjoyed this book and had some fun and laughs on every page. If you did, please think about leaving a review for us on Amazon or wherever you purchased this book. It may only take a moment, but it really does mean the world for small businesses like mine.

Our mission is to create premium content for children that will help them build confidence, grow their imaginations, get away from screens, spend more quality time with family, and have lots of fun and laughs doing it. Without you, however, this would not be possible, so we sincerely thank you for your purchase and for supporting our company mission.
~ Hayden

Check out our other books!

For more, visit our Amazon store at:
amazon.com/author/haydenfox

Made in the USA
Middletown, DE
05 December 2020

26447637R00040